IT'S TIME TO EAT MILKSHAKES

It's Time to Eat MILKSHAKES

Walter the Educator

Silent King Books
A WhichHead Entertainment Imprint

Copyright © 2024 by Walter the Educator

All rights reserved. No part of this book may be reproduced in any manner whatsoever without written per- mission except in the case of brief quotations embodied in critical articles and reviews.

First Printing, 2024

Disclaimer

This book is a literary work; the story is not about specific persons, locations, situations, and/or circumstances unless mentioned in a historical context. Any resemblance to real persons, locations, situations, and/or circumstances is coincidental. This book is for entertainment and informational purposes only. The author and publisher offer this information without warranties expressed or implied. No matter the grounds, neither the author nor the publisher will be accountable for any losses, injuries, or other damages caused by the reader's use of this book. The use of this book acknowledges an understanding and acceptance of this disclaimer.

It's Time to Eat MILKSHAKES is a collectible early learning book by Walter the Educator suitable for all ages belonging to Walter the Educator's Time to Eat Book Series. Collect more books at WaltertheEducator.com

USE THE EXTRA SPACE TO TAKE NOTES AND DOCUMENT YOUR MEMORIES

MILKSHAKES

It's time for a treat so cold and sweet,

It's Time to Eat
Milkshakes

A Thai milkshake that's fun to eat!

Creamy and thick, with colors bright,

A sip of joy that feels just right.

In a tall cup, smooth and cool,

Thai milkshakes make us drool!

Flavors that pop, from tea to fruit,

Every sip is a tasty hoot.

Sometimes orange, sometimes pink,

These colorful shakes are fun to drink!

We swirl the straw, give it a spin,

And watch the colors mix right in.

With creamy milk and tasty ice,

Each sip feels cool, smooth, and nice.

A hint of sweet, a little spice,

Every taste is just precise.

It's Time to Eat
Milkshakes

Some have fruit, like mango or lime,

Each milkshake flavor feels so fine!

From top to bottom, thick and cold,

Each sip is a story to be told.

We take big gulps, we take it slow,

This tasty shake makes us glow!

A frosty drink on a sunny day,

Thai milkshakes take us away.

With ice that clinks and flavors that cheer,

These tasty shakes bring us near.

For family and friends, a tasty blend,

A Thai milkshake is our new friend!

Sometimes with bubbles that bounce inside,

Or little jellies that twist and glide.

It's Time to Eat
Milkshakes

Every sip brings something new,

A magic drink for me and you!

So gather 'round and take a taste,

No time for this shake to go to waste!

With every sip, our smiles grow wide,

Thai milkshakes fill us with pride.

It's Time to Eat
Milkshakes

From the first sip to the very end,

This creamy shake is our best friend!

A chilly, sweet, delightful cheer

It's Time to Eat
Milkshakes

Thai milkshakes, we hold so dear!

ABOUT THE CREATOR

Walter the Educator is one of the pseudonyms for Walter Anderson. Formally educated in Chemistry, Business, and Education, he is an educator, an author, a diverse entrepreneur, and he is the son of a disabled war veteran. "Walter the Educator" shares his time between educating and creating. He holds interests and owns several creative projects that entertain, enlighten, enhance, and educate, hoping to inspire and motivate you. Follow, find new works, and stay up to date with Walter the Educator™

at WaltertheEducator.com